POLE
POSITION

First published in 2025 by OH
An Imprint of HEADLINE PUBLISHING GROUP

1

Disclaimer:
This book has not been licensed, approved, sponsored, or endorsed by Lando Norris

Lando Norris is a registered trademark owned by Lando Norris, 1 Rue de la Lujerneta, c/o The Office, Monaco, MC-98000

Cataloguing in Publication Data is available from the British Library

ISBN 978-1-03543-309-4

Compiled and written by: David Clayton
Editorial: Matt Tomlinson
Designed and typset in Queulat by: Stephen Cary
Project manager: Russell Porter
Illustration by: Ryan Adley
Production: Rachel Burgess
Printed and bound in Dubai

Headline's policy is to use papers that are natural, renewable and recyclable products and made from wood grown in well-managed forests and other controlled sources. The logging and manufacturing processes are expected to conform to the environmental regulations of the country of origin.

HEADLINE PUBLISHING GROUP LIMITED
An Hachette UK Company
Carmelite House, 50 Victoria Embankment, London EC4Y 0DZ

The authorised representative in the EEA is Hachette Ireland, 8 Castlecourt Centre, Dublin 15, D15 XTP3, Ireland (email: info@hbgi.ie)

www.headline.co.uk www.hachette.co.uk

POLE POSITION

THE LITTLE GUIDE TO

LANDO NORRIS

UNOFFICIAL AND UNAUTHORIZED

CONTENTS

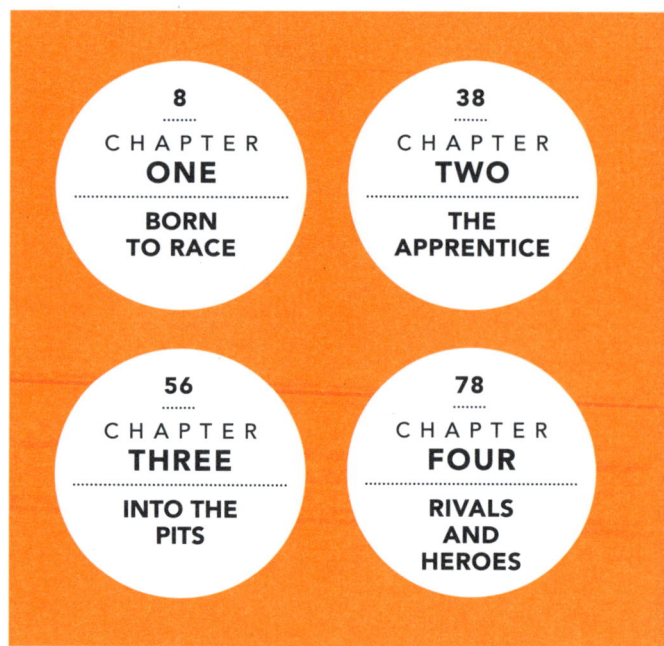

INTRODUCTION

Whether he was riding at full speed on the family's sit-on mower, driving old bangers with his dad or even riding horses, Lando Norris has always had a thirst for speed and competing. Inspired by his hero – world champion motorcyclist Valentino Rossi – young Lando wanted to go fast or go home. Supported by his family, the youngster was encouraged to try go-karting – and never looked back.

He would sacrifice his education, friends and teenage years to follow his dreams, racing, competing and practising endlessly in a home simulator to become the best he could be. His privileged upbringing gave him the opportunity to follow his dream until he gradually began to stand on his own two feet as karting turned to Formulas 4, 3 and then 2, and the young Brit emerged as one of the outstanding young talents of his generation.

In 2017, McLaren signed him up as a young driver, before promoting him to be their official test and reserve driver for the 2018 season.

In 2019, he signed a contract to compete in Formula 1 for McLaren and has become one of motorsport's most popular and charismatic figures, with his playful, often outspoken, persona revealed – and embraced by a new, younger audience of F1 fans.

He is already spoken about as one of the true British F1 greats, and his future continues to look bright... orange.

CHAPTER
ONE

Born to Race

From the moment he could walk, Lando Norris was obsessed with anything that moved fast.

He idolised Valentino Rossi, and initially it looked like bikes would be his obsession – until he discovered the family lawn-mower, and then go-karts...

"

Initially what got me into
Valentino was just his colours.
I was probably only five years
old at the time, and when
you're at that age it's hard
to like anything for a reason
other than it looked cool!

"

*Lando Norris on nine-time motorcycle world
champion Valentino Rossi, his first inspiration to
race, formula 1.com, October 2023.*

"

When I was about six
I got a motorcross
bike, because I was
quite into motorbikes
watching MotoGP, and
my hero at the time
was Valentino Rossi.

"

*On how he was initially more interested in two
wheels than four, International Journal of
the FIA, #21, 2017.*

"

I'd sit on his lap, and we'd just tear around on this thing. What's the worst Citroën? A Saxo or something? He bought it for about £200 and it would overheat in 10 minutes!

"

Lando remembers driving around a field in Glastonbury with his dad in an old banger getting a taste for speed, The Telegraph, July 2024.

"

I used to love driving the mower. It was a proper sit-on one. But I was so small when I was a kid – 30kg when I was 10 – I had to drag some of my dad's dumbbells from some old gym equipment he had and put them on the mower, because the mower wouldn't start unless there was 50kg on top. I used to go out after school and just drive the mower and cut everything and perfect the garden!

"

On how high-speed gardening scratched an early itch, The Telegraph, July 2024.

FACT

Lando sampled kart racing for the first time at Clay Pigeon Raceway aged seven, along with older brother Oliver, and began competing in karting races soon afterwards.

Bonus fact:

Former F1 world champion Jenson Button also first raced at Clay Pigeon.

> "
> First day of school is boring but it's May Fair so not so bad plus my mum is making pancakes yum, yum.
> "

A 13-year-old Lando's Tweet from 2012 would come back to haunt him years later, sportskeeda.com, March 2022.

"

One day after school my dad
took me and my brother to the
local kart track, which was
Clay Pigeon, for a round of the
British Super 1 Championship.
As soon as I saw it, I told my dad
that I wanted to have a go.

"

*On his early beginnings, redbull.com,
December 2016.*

66

I wasn't hugely into motor racing when I was younger, I never really watched every Formula One race, I just watched a few. When I started karting I started watching more and more and got more interested in Formula One.

99

Lando on an interest that grew into an obsession, sportsjournalismsgs.com, January 2017.

66

I think when I was super young, I loved [school]. Like all kids, you love it. And you have a lot of friends and stuff. But when I started travelling a little bit – by the time I was eight I was racing properly – I would start to miss a bit of school. And I think as soon as you have that, at such a young age, it already

starts to affect you. And it only gets worse. The more you step up, the more you travel, the more you go away, the longer the weekends are, you're travelling to Europe... and that age is when most people make childhood friends, some of which last a lifetime.

"

Lando explains how racing affected his education, The Telegraph, July 2024.

"

I missed so much. I remember missing the first week in September and arriving after everyone had already settled in. And I'm like: I don't really know anyone here. And I'm late. And then I'm there for three days, and then I'm gone again. I just never really settled.

"

Lando recalls more about schooling issues, The Telegraph, July 2024.

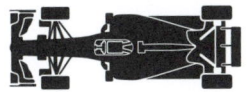

"

The racing is quite boring, sometimes. It's hard to see how it pulls in fans. The races compared to other categories are sometimes a lot worse, they should always be better.

"

Lando wasn't overly enamoured with F1 as a youngster, Daily Mail, March 2018.

"

I've never been shy to admit the help and support I've had from my family and from my dad growing up. Him supporting me, being able to be with good teams always – like, anyone would if they were in that same position. I was very lucky that my dad was able to support me and do it.

"

Lando being honest and open about his privileged upbringing, racefans.net, September 2023.

"

The turning point was when I started racing. I would be racing at weekends – more and more often as I progressed up the ladder. Soon travelling to Europe and then around the world.

"

Lando on how he got the racing bug,
thegentlemansjournal.com, 2020.

"

I was tiny as a kid,
so I just wasn't that
confident. My whole life
was racing. Whenever
I was at school I was
watching racing videos
and sitting on my own.

"

On his lonely school life, The Telegraph, July 2024.

66

I knew that this was what
I wanted to do by the time I was
13. By then, I could think for
myself, and I knew what
I wanted. Before that, all of the
stuff I had been doing was for
fun, and I never thought that it
was what I was going to do for
a career, for a life.

99

On realising his true aspirations,
thegentlemansjournal.com, July 2024.

66

If I want to do well in
racing I need to be more
focused, so I stopped going
to school. If I wasn't a very
good driver it would not
be a wise decision, but it
gives me an advantage
over my competitors.

99

On making crucial decisions, motorsport.co.uk, 2017.

I am absolutely my own biggest critic.

On his self-critical mentality, The Guardian, March 2019.

"

I think the main one for me was probably the world championship in karting. I wasn't the fastest at all really on that weekend, I was just pretty good, but we basically never gave up, kept fighting throughout the weekend, and yeah I mean obviously to come away as a world champion is something pretty cool.

"

On becoming a karting world champion at the age of 13, sportsjournalismsgs.com, January 2017.

FACT

Lando's father made his fortune in pensions and at one stage was one of the 500 wealthiest men in the UK.

That enabled Lando to make choices perhaps other kids couldn't, and he was allowed to leave school before his GCSE exams and instead spend up to 14 hours a day on a racing simulator at his Glastonbury home.

> **"**
> I'm a competitive guy, so if I can beat other drivers in whatever it is, that's just an added bonus.
> **"**

On what drives him, GQ, January 2018.

66

I'm very excited to be joining Carlin and can't wait to contest the Formula 3 European Championship. My aim is simple and the same as at the start of every season – I want to win the championship title outright.

99

Lando sets out his F3 targets, autosport.com, December 2016.

"

Although it's my rookie F3
season, I'm totally confident
with the package – the team
and Volkswagen. I believe I
have what it takes to challenge
for the title in my first full
season of F3 racing.

"

On his F3 aspirations, somersetlive.co.uk,
April 2017.

FACT

A 17-year-old Lando Norris became the then youngest winner of the prestigious European Formula Three Championship, sealing the title with two rounds to go.

"

There are going to be things I'm not going to be great at, times when I make mistakes, 100%.

"

On accepting mistakes and learning from them, BBC, February 2019.

66

I would never want
to pay to come into F1.
I would never want my
dad to have done that.
I personally just don't
see that as the most
deserving way of being
in Formula 1.

99

Lando shows he's always been determined to find his own way into Formula 1, despite his family's wealth, racefans.net, September 2023.

"

I made that deal with my dad.
We made it so that he wouldn't
pay for me to get into Formula 1.
And that's how it went. I ended
up joining McLaren. I won the
British Young Driver Award.
I ended up then getting my
simulator role with the team and
getting my first pay cheque.

"

Lando on finding his own path,
racefans.net, September 2023.

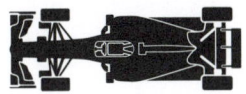

66

Yeah that's the aim:
to win championships
in Formula One.

99

On his ultimate goal, sportingjournalism.com, 2017.

CHAPTER
TWO

The Apprentice

As he moved through various levels in motorsport, Lando was honing his craft, learning his trade and starting to get noticed in wider circles.

The bright, bubbly West Country lad had big dreams... and the talent to fulfil them.

"

I wasn't bullied or anything.
I just never really integrated.
I missed that growing-up period.
I never went out. Never partied.
And then by the time I was 18,
I was almost in Formula 1. And
then you're like, 'OK, be a good
boy,' and all of that.

"

Lando Norris on missing out on his teenage years,
The Telegraph, July 2024.

FACT

In February 2017, McLaren added Lando to their young driver roster and gave him his first official F1 test at the Hungaroring in August of that year.

The young Brit impressed immediately and set the second-quickest time of the day. Three months later, McLaren confirmed Lando would be their test and reserve driver for 2018.

66

Fernando Alonso, one of the best racing drivers in the world, [and] Lando was his match.

99

Zak Brown, CEO of McLaren racing, on comparing Lando and Alonso at the Daytona 24 Hours race in 2018, BBC, March 2025.

"

I was patient,
but I always felt like
I wanted to be ahead
of where I was.

"

*Lando on his wait to become one of McLaren's
competing drivers, GQ, January 2023.*

FACT

*Having finished second
(to George Russell)
in the 2018
F2 Championship,
Lando Norris was
announced as a McLaren
Formula 1 driver for
the 2019 season.*

> **"**
> I think as long as I do a good job and put in all my effort to proving that I'm worth it, then everything should be fine.
> **"**

An 18-year-old Lando ahead of his first F1 season, BBC, September 2018.

66

The mental health side of things is something I struggled a lot with, especially in my first year of Formula 1, with the pressure and the nerves and social media and things like that.

99

Lando looks back on a tough rookie year in F1,
Radio Times, July 2021.

"

It's cool because I was a nobody, years ago, now I can have this positive impact on people. I can help people. It's something you don't often think about. I want to be a driver, like that's always the dream, but then it's knowing I can be a driver who has this impact on people and help people out, to make them feel better. I'm definitely glad I opened up and spoke about things publicly.

"

On his new role and the power that comes with it,
Radio Times, July 2021.

"

When people think my ego is too big or something, it couldn't be further from the truth – especially when I'm driving. Maybe sometimes I choose the wrong words or something, and people somehow use that against me.

"

On how he may be misunderstood by the media, therace.com, November 2024.

FACT

Partnered with Carlos Sainz Jr, in Lando's debut F1 season he helped McLaren to finish fourth in the Constructors' Championship, as they more than doubled the previous year's points.

Sainz collected more points, but Lando qualified ahead of his teammate 11 times. His best finish in his rookie year was sixth in Bahrain.

"

I've always hated to use 'experience' as an excuse. I never wanted to say, 'He beat me today because of experience.' I dreaded that. But you can't prepare for every single thing in the world in that first race, and you realise that with time that you do gain experience, and you make fewer mistakes.

"

On learning his trade, GQ, January 2023.

" I'm an all-or-nothing kind of guy, I guess. "

On his winning mentality, GQ, March 2019.

> **"**
>
> I like the tracks that are more technical, for example, Singapore, Monaco, Spa or Suzuka. And I'm really excited to be back racing now it's safe to do so!
>
> **"**

Lando on the return to F1 racing as the pandemic eases, thegentlemansjournal, August 2020.

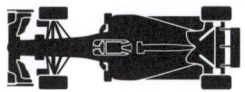

" FU*KKKK YEAHHHHH! "

Lando celebrates third place – his first podium finish – at the 2020 Austrian Grand Prix on his Instagram page (@lando), July 2020.

"

I'm done with the podiums... bored of them.

"

A frustrated Lando chases that elusive first F1 victory, The Standard, March 2022.

66

About time! What a race. It's been a long time coming, but finally I've managed to do it. I'm so happy for my whole team, I finally delivered for them. A long day, tough race, but finally on top, so I'm over the moon.

99

Lando finally breaks his F1 duck with a maiden victory at the 2024 Miami Grand Prix, formula1.com, May 2024.

C H A P T E R

THREE

Into the Pits

The life of a Formula 1 driver
is not without struggles –
whether with cars, the team
or life in general – and Lando
Norris is no stranger to the
occasional set-back...

"

Generally, if it's smoke, it's something quite bad. If it's on a race day, and through no fault of my own the engine lets go when everyone's put so much work in... yeah, it's such a big letdown to not be able to finish the race. That's part of racing. It happens to every driver at some point. It's happened to Lewis, it's happened to Lando.

"

Lando explains what a bad day for a F1 driver looks like, GQ, January 2023.

"

I would love to be able to drive another car [other than a McLaren] just to go, 'OK, that's what a difference can be.' I feel like last year to this year is also a very big difference, so I don't know how much bigger it's going to be.

"

On wondering about what another car might be like, therace.com, October 2023.

"

I think I'm a fair loser, but
I've always been a guy who's very
harsh on myself. I'm very critical
of my own performance. I always
think, 'What could I have done
better?' And then, 'What could
the team have done better?'

"

On learning from mistakes,
The Mirror, January 2023.

"

When I came into F1, I wanted to go out and do the perfect lap straight away. Now I have the faith that I can try a lot of different things and then I can go into qualifying and piece it all together. That's something I wouldn't have been able to do in year one or year two, because I wouldn't have been able to try so many things by not having [always] tried to do a perfect lap.

"

On learning his trade as he goes along,
therace.com, October 2023.

"

I hate losing. But losing gives me the drive to figure it out and do a better job next time.

"

On learning from adversity, GQ, January 2023.

66

Getting the team around you is so important. Growing up, I heard about how good [Michael] Schumacher was at it. To get everyone on his side, overcoming his teammate, that's how it is with all the best drivers. It's not just about driving, it's about working as a team to develop the car, evolving it race by race across the whole season.

99

On being inclusive and a team player, GQ, March 2019.

66

F2 cars have downforce; they're quick. But it's difficult for your brain and eyes to keep up with everything that's going on once you're in an F1 car. You get used to it and you learn to stay calm, because if you react too quickly the opposite will happen. Being more relaxed is when it becomes more natural and controlled.

99

On keeping control of the beast he is in charge of, GQ, March 2019.

66

If it didn't rain any more, I'm 99.999% sure I would've won the race. The only person who would've beaten me was Lewis if he managed to get past. And when he boxed [pitted], if it didn't rain any more, I'm 100% sure I would've won the race – he wouldn't have been able to catch me.

99

Lando reacts to being overtaken by Lewis Hamilton and being denied a first F1 win at the 2021 Russian Grand Prix, BBC, November 2021.

"

It's been very cool to get to know them a bit more. Every now and again, I speak to Lewis on the parade laps and stuff like that. I guess because I still see them as more established drivers. Definitely [it] just boosts your confidence when you hear things from them because they've experienced every situation that I'm learning or have gone through this season.

"

On being accepted by other drivers,
BBC, November 2021.

"

I was watching them
on TV when I was, like,
seven years old, so it's
rewarding and cool to
hear it from someone like
that, people I looked up
to for many years.

"

*More from Lando on rubbing shoulders with
F1's greats, BBC, November 2021.*

66

I feel like I'm really relaxed and chilled in the car but then I'm always the opposite when I listen to myself afterwards.

99

Lando bemoans his vocalisation when driving, Sky Sports, August 2023.

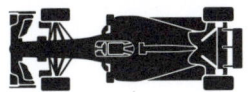

"

My goal is always to push
a little bit harder and keep
looking forward. Formula 1
is constantly evolving,
and so am I. Every lap,
every corner is a chance
to perfect my craft.

"

*Lando allows a glimpse into his racing
mentality, readthis.uk, January 2025.*

66

When that realisation kind of
sets in of 'it's gone', it's a tough
one. This is what I've done since
I was a kid, this is all I want to do.
So, as soon as that kind of candle
is gone and it's over, it hurts.

99

Lando on his reaction to losing the 2024 Drivers'
Championship, Daily Express, January 2025.

"

I definitely don't go around and joke and laugh as much as I used to, and I think people loved that and maybe don't like it as much now I don't.

"

On his shift in gears from the joker to champion-elect, therace.com, November 2024.

66

I've always been honest
when I've done a good job and
done a bad job. When I know
I've done something wrong,
or someone tells me I've done
something wrong, I'll always
accept it and acknowledge
that in the right way.

99

*On the importance of honesty, and
sometimes having to accept criticism,
therace.com, November 2024.*

"

There's some kind of
stuff I don't understand,
especially the amount
of negative stuff I get
nowadays – I almost want
to say for no reason.
It puzzles me a little bit.

"

*Lando coming to terms with the price of
fame, therace.com, November 2024.*

"

It might be that I'm happier living life a little bit more on the edge...

"

On embracing risk, therace.com, February 2023.

"

[I'm] disappointed, of course. I've let the team down. The team gave me a great car today, easily the quickest out there, and I f*cked it up.

"

Lando on his 10-second stop-go penalty at the 2024 Qatar Grand Prix, formula1.com, December 2024.

66

You know, I'm not an idiot.
If there's a yellow flag, I know
I need to slow down. That's
rule number one you learn in
go-karts. For some reason
I didn't do that today because
I've not seen it or missed it or
something, so I have to take it
on the chin.

99

More from Lando on his 10-second stop-go penalty
at the 2024 Qatar Grand Prix, autosport.com,
December 2024.

66

I've disappointed
the whole team, and
the only thing I care
about is my team.

99

*Lando continues to chide himself on his error
at the 2024 Qatar Grand Prix, therace.com,
December 2024.*

CHAPTER
FOUR

Rivals and Heroes

Lando Norris doesn't hold back with his opinions – if another driver's actions anger him, he calls them out.

But he also has close friends and people he admires, as well as love/hate relationships with some of F1's biggest names...

"

Carlos and I get on extremely well. I kind of grew up with him. Daniel I got on with pretty well. He and I were the perfect competitors: we hated beating each other like we hated getting beat by one another.

"

Lando on his reported tensions with fellow drivers Carlos Sainz Jr and Daniel Ricciardo, GQ, January 2023.

66

Destroy him? Do I?
I have to beat him.
It's rule number one,
really – beating
your teammate.

99

Lando responds to how he needs to compete with McLaren teammate Carlo Sainz Jr, GQ, March 2019.

"

I'd love it if we could battle George and Mercedes for championships and wins. I look forward to that time.

"

On his hopes of rekindling his junior racing rivalry with fellow Brit George Russell, Daily Express, March 2022.

"

It's always competitive between teammates. We get on well, we still have good laughs every now and then, doing fun interviews and things. It's different to Carlos [Sainz], my old teammate, just a different vibe, because Dan is a bit older and has a lot more experience within Formula 1 but there's a lot of things I've been able to learn from him.

"

On his teammate Daniel Ricciardo, Radio Times, July 2021.

"

I keep it separate; I can be the biggest competitor I need to be on the race track, but I can also respect and be good mates with other people.

"

On being a different beast on the track, GQ, January 2023.

"

Everyone has to admire [Hamilton's] pace, especially in qualifying. He is a driver I support, in terms of him being British, and I want him to win, but he isn't an idol to me.

"

On being an admirer of Lewis Hamilton but nothing more, Daily Mail, November 2017.

"

He obviously didn't learn
from Friday, but he doesn't
seem to learn from anything
he does. It happens a lot with
him, so I just need to stay
away. It wasn't a nice battle.
I don't know what I'm meant
to say... he crashes a lot.

"

*Lando reacts angrily to Lance Stroll's
performance in the 2020 Portuguese
Grand Prix, Sky Sports, October 2020.*

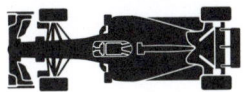

66

I don't know if he can't
see properly in the right side or
something. He ruined his own
race, he ruined my race, it was
his fault. He didn't need to risk
what he did – I don't know why
he tried to be a hero.

99

*More from Lando on Stroll's seemingly reckless
drive in Portugal, Sky Sports, October 2020.*

"

My first apology was more for the language I used more than anything. Not everything I said I apologised for but just the specific wording of what I said.

"

Lando apologises for some of the comments he made after the Portuguese Grand Prix, autosport.com, October 2020.

66

It doesn't mean anything to me, really. He's in a car which should win every race, basically.

99

Lando is asked post-race what Lewis Hamilton's landmark 92nd win means to him personally after the 2020 Portuguese Grand Prix and sets social media alight, Sky Sport, October 2020.

66

I owe an apology. I've been stupid and careless with some things I've said lately in media and interviews and haven't shown the respect I should have to certain people. I'm not that kind of person, so know I should apologise to them but also everyone reading/ listening. Sorry.

99

Lando takes to Twitter to apologise to Lewis Hamilton, Twitter/X, October 2020.

66

I woke up in the morning and I looked on social media and there was a lot more bad comments than good about the things I said. I never meant any of it to be put in that way or taken out of context in a bad way, especially against Lewis. So I made the decision in the morning to put out the tweet and just issue my apology. And message Lewis also at the same time to set things straight.

99

Lando backtracks on his ill-chosen words about Lewis Hamilton, formula1.com, October 2020.

"

The [apology] was more [for the]
comments about Lewis, and him
reaching his 92 wins, which
I have a lot of respect for, and
I didn't choose the right words to
put it into context.

"

*More from Lando as he sets the record
straight, formula1.com, October 2020.*

"

The last few days have probably been the worst; I am a nice guy really.

"

*Lando reels from the social media backlash
to his Hamilton and Stroll comments,
essentiallysports.com, October 2020.*

"

It ended well, it didn't
start well. There was a
complete contrast,
I think. Possibly the worst
start of my career ever,
probably the worst start of
everyone's career ever.

"

*Lando's slightly over-the-top assertion of his
topsy-turvy 2020 Turkish Grand Prix, where he
eventually rescued an eighth-place finish,
motorsport.com, November 2020.*

"

I don't know where it came from. We've been confident all weekend and been doing a good job and the car has been much nicer this weekend than it was last weekend – so we understand some things.

"

Lando is surprised at his own performance after grabbing fourth on the grid ahead of the 2020 Abu Dhabi Grand Prix, Sky Sports, December 2020.

> **I don't deserve three points on my licence for this. I didn't do anything dangerous. I didn't do anything because I didn't know, or I was clueless.**

Lando argues his punishment at the 2021 Azerbaijan Grand Prix was unjust, racefans.net, June 2021.

"

Max just placed it too close to the edge. It fell over, I guess. Not my problem. It's his!

"

Lando jokes the damage sustained to the $45,000 winner's trophy at the Hungarian Grand Prix was down to winner Verstappen's placement rather than his signature podium bang with a champagne bottle, motorsport.com, July 2023.

"

I always say things that I...
When you look at it after,
I always make myself look like
an idiot and I get that, but the
people that I speak to know that
I would never mean something
like that, of course.

"

*Lando's regret at his expletive-filled radio rant at what
he believed was his engineer's poor strategy at the
2023 Dutch Grand Prix, Sky Sports, August 2023.*

"

A bit of it is just emotions at the time. I always sound like I'm crying or I'm moaning on the radio. I don't know why, I hate it.

"

More from Lando after the 2023 Dutch Grand Prix, Sky Sports, August 2023.

"

He saw me after, and he came up to congratulate me, so I guess it's an honour. Whenever you have someone like this come up to you to take time out of their life to pay their respect for what you've done... it has to be an honour.

"

Lando on meeting then President-elect Donald Trump after winning the Miami Grand Prix, Daily Mail, May 2024.

"

Congrats on the 4th title in a row mate, awesome drive this year. Was fun fighting you for it. Feels like yesterday we took this pic in karting.

"

Lando's caption on a picture of him and Max Verstappen as kids after the Dutchman claimed his fourth world title in Las Vegas, Daily Mail, November 2024.

"

It's a pretty cool thing I have
so much respect for him and
what he's been able to achieve in
F1. He's part of the reason I'm an
F1 driver, so it's weird thinking
I'm now racing against him.

"

*Lando talks about his admiration
for Lewis Hamilton, BBC, July 2023.*

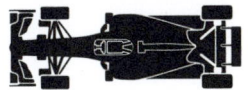

"

I am not always the guy who asks a lot of questions to these kind of people to get to know what they're like and what they think. I do it in a more subtle way and just try to understand how they think and their thought processes and kind of understand what makes them special.

"

*More from Lando on getting to know
Lewis Hamilton, BBC, July 2023.*

66

Lewis Hamilton: *Phew, you guys
are fast.*
Lando Norris: *You had a fast car
seven years ago...*
Hamilton: *Seven years ago? Long time.
Were you here seven years ago?*
Norris: *Yeah, well, you had a quick car, you
made the most of it, and now it's us.*
Hamilton: *I wasn't complaining, I was
just complimenting your car.*

99

*Slightly awkward exchange between Lando and
Lewis in the cooldown room after the 2024
Hungarian Grand Prix, planetf1.com, July 2024.*

66

Mercedes were on pole here
last year, and their car has
been pretty good. I know Lewis
complains a lot of how amazing
our car is and how bad theirs is,
but they don't have a bad car.
And they haven't all season.

99

Back on the offensive against Hamilton,
Daily Express, July 2024.

"

Yesterday, Lewis complained of how tough it was finishing outside first position. Try racing in 19th and 20th. He's never done that in his life. So that's the only thing that Lewis hasn't done in Formula 1.

"

At it again! Daily Express, July 2024.

"

If you look at Barcelona, when
I had a 'bad' start everyone
says, the best starter in that
race was Max. And I think
I was like the third or fourth
best starter on the grid. It's just
I happened to be next to the
guy who got the best start.

"

Lando laments being (nearly) alongside
Max Verstappen at the 2024 Spanish Grand
Prix, therace.com, November 2024.

> **"**
>
> I absolutely think I can go up against Max and give him a good challenge. But I also rate Max; it's extremely difficult for anyone to challenge him for a world championship.
>
> **"**

On competing with his best buddy,
The Guardian, April 2024.

"
It's not talent,
it's just luck.
"

Lando's frosty description of Max Verstappen's
2024 Brazilian Grand Prix win from seventeenth on
the grid, racefans.net, November 2024.

66

First of all, I retract that comment back there, where I said it was all luck, no talent. You know how the media changes things. But first of all, congratulations to Max. What he did this year, and what he did in Brazil this year, was incredible. So I'm the first one to acknowledge such a thing when I'm the one going up against him.

99

Lando retracts his comments about Verstappen at the FIA Gala, The Sun, December 2024.

"

He was the guy who, when I was such a young kid, I looked up to and I dreamt of being like him in many ways. There are still things and characteristics that maybe I have which are similar to him, like my helmet design and the colours, and just things I like to do. He was the guy that inspired me to be who I am today.

"

On hero Valentino Rossi's influence on his career, crash.net, March 2022.

CHAPTER
FIVE

What They Said...

From high praise to good advice, observations on his abilities to relief at a first win, here's what the great and good of Formula 1 have said about the British driver...

"

I think we get the best
out of him; he's more
talkative and engaged.
He's able to let his hair
down. It's like family.

"

*McLaren CEO Zak Brown on coaxing Lando
to be more confident, GQ, January 2023.*

"

When he first went up against Fernando Alonso it was like another day at the office. I think that calmness and coolness is why he's so consistent.

"

McLaren CEO Zak Brown on Lando's calm persona when competing, GQ, January 2023.

"

What frustrates me about Lando? He's been five minutes late more than once. If we're supposed to leave at 8:00, it might be 8:07. The great thing about him is he is very honest and owns everything. And he's definitely improved.

"

Zak Brown on Lando's penchant for tardiness, GQ, January 2023.

66

He had pretty much won everything he'd ever sat in at a very young age, and in his first time doing it. All of that means he's an extremely special talent.

99

Brown explains his decision to sign Norris to McLaren in 2017, GQ, January 2023.

"

Lando has impressed us since his rookie year with his performances, and his evolution as a driver since then has been clear to see. He's an integral part of our performance recovery plan and his record so far, securing two podiums with the team over the past year, has shown he's a formidable competitor on track.

"

Then McLaren team principal Andreas Seidl on the decision to retain Lando's services in 2022, BBC, May 2021.

"

There's no reason why he shouldn't be the favourite, right? Because at the end of this year, McLaren was the strongest car. He has been marginally stronger than Piastri within the team. So he should be the favourite.

"

Nico Rosberg, 2016 champion, on Lando's chances of winning the 2025 Drivers' Championship, Sky Sports' The F1 Show podcast, February 2025.

"

He needs a little bit of help from Ferrari, to take points away from Max. I don't think he has really at the moment understood what is possible. He hasn't got that nastiness in him yet, like Max Verstappen has. Once he gets used to winning, he will grow that.

"

Former Haas boss, and bestselling author, Guenther Steiner on why Lando needs to get meaner, The Standard, October 2024.

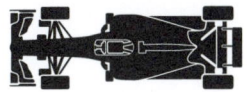

"

He knows how to get the best out of a race car and put the car to its limits. He's also able to very articulately convey what that car is doing, because he has such a good feel for it; his technical feedback is excellent.

"

Zak Brown on Lando's main strengths, GQ, January 2023.

"

There's a lot of people on the bandwagon criticising Max [Verstappen] for this, that and the other. But I would just say one thing, that he's a very, very young boy Lando [Norris]. He is an incredible talent and will be in the future, but one thing he has to learn and what yesterday will have taught him is that Max is a fighter, he's a bear.

"

Eddie Jordan on the battle Lando faces to be world champion, f1oversteer.com, July 2024.

"

Norris will learn a lot from this. If you haven't had that experience of starting at the front before, this is something you have to learn. You also notice that that pressure was there because he didn't even want to talk about the title situation for a while. He didn't have good starts either, but he learned. He definitely learned.

"

Former F1 world champion Mario Andretti on how Lando can become a champion, f1oversteer.com, February 2025.

FACT

Lando Norris became the 21st British driver to win a world championship Grand Prix and the 114th in total.

His May 2024 win in Miami saw him tie with Patrick Depailler, Jean Alesi, Mika Häkkinen and Eddie Irvine for the most podium finishes before a first win (15) on his 110th start for McLaren.

"

A massive well done to Lando and McLaren. He truly deserves it, and all told, he probably deserves to have more than one victory already by now. We've been racing each other for a long time – he's put so much hard work in, and I had no doubts that he would win in F1. I'm very happy for him.

"

Long-time friend (and rival) George Russell congratulates Lando on his first win, formula1.com, May 2024.

"

I am so happy for Lando and McLaren. They have both been doing a great job and they deserve today's victory. It's great to see McLaren so competitive. I also know how special it is to get your first Grand Prix victory, so a big well done to Lando.

"

Praise from one of the sport's legends, Lewis Hamilton, in Miami, formula1.com, May 2024.

"

We do have some work to do
to improve our performance
in the next couple of races.
I am happy for Lando.
It's always special to secure
your first win.

"

*Fernando Alonso, another legend, on Lando's
first win, formula1.com, May 2024.*

> ❝
>
> I'm very happy for Lando.
> It's been a long time coming.
> And it's not going to be his
> last one. He definitely deserves
> it today.
>
> ❞

Lando's big rival of 2024, Max Verstappen,
is full of praise, formula1.com, May 2024.

66

I'm also genuinely happy for Lando; big congratulations to him. He is a rival but also a friend. I know how talented he is and I knew it was just a matter of time for him to take his first win.

99

Daniel Ricciardo, Lando's former teammate, on Lando's first win, formula1.com, May 2024.

"

Well, first of all, I'm really happy for Lando. He deserves it. Very often, he arrived very close to it, but for one reason or another, he didn't make it. But today, he did an incredible job, and the whole weekend he has been on it.

"

Charles Leclerc on Lando's win in Miami, formula1.com, May 2024.

"

I think he's got another 10 to
15 years ahead of him. I think
as long as we can get him a
car, he'll be a world champion.

"

Zak Brown on Lando's potential longevity,
Sports Illustrated, January 2023.

"

Congratulations to Lando, I'm truly happy for him! He deserved a win for a long time and today was his day.

"

Another former teammate, Carlos Sainz, offers his congratulations, formula1.com, May 2024.

> **Well Lando, it's a fantastic victory. I think I might have a solution if you're feeling dizzy...**

Sky Sports presenter and former F1 star David Coulthard drenches Lando with water after Lando mentions he feels a "little dizzy" after his win in Singapore, The Sun, September 2024.

CHAPTER

SIX

Off Track

Occasionally, we get a glimpse into the world of a young F1 star's life away from the high-octane world of racing at ridiculous speed...

66

I've never wanted to go out and get wrecked. But I can't just drink a little. If I do it, I have to go all the way. I'm an all-or-nothing kind of guy, I guess.

99

Lando has the same attitude off the track as he does on it, GQ, March 2019.

"

I don't really drink at the best of times. If I ever win a race they are going to have to find me something other than Champagne as I cannot stand the stuff.

"

Lando reveals his dislike of the traditional race winner's tipple, The Telegraph, June 2022.

> 66
>
> # We get drug-tested like every freaking week.
>
> 99

Lando clears up any rumours about his downtime, The Telegraph, June 2024.

> **"**
>
> Now more and more I fly my friends out, so we can play some golf together, or just hang out. Otherwise, again, you just get more and more isolated.
>
> **"**

On avoiding lonelines, The Telegraph, June 2024.

"

I definitely care too much about people's perceptions of me. I certainly think I cared way too much when I started out in like 2019–20, though I care less now. Some people are going to like you, some aren't. They can have whatever perception they want. You just have to accept that.

"

On trying to deal with the haters,
The Telegraph, June 2024.

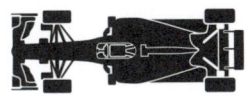

"

I have quite specific things I need to eat. I lack in some areas with my diet as I'm not a big foodie. I mean, I love food, but I'm quite picky, so I need to eat particular things to keep myself in good shape. I work hard with my trainer to make sure my diet is very tailored to what my body needs.

"

On maintaining a good diet and health regime, thegentlemansjournal.com, 2020.

"

Favourite food? Belgian chocolate! Or chips with a bit of mayonnaise. That's always the one thing you must have when you go to Belgium.

"

On his Belgian food favourites,
thegentlemansjournal.com, 2020.

"

I actually still consider Spa in Belgium one of my home tracks. Split with Silverstone. Because I'm definitely 50/50 — although I don't speak a lot of Flemish. I love both places and have family in both. It's just a cool thing to have.

"

On his dual nationality and split loyalties, thegentlemansjournal.com, 2020.

> **❝**
>
> Thanks to all my viewers for raising over $12,000 by the end total for Twitch Stream Aid and the fight against COVID-19. I do have to cut all my hair off now though...
>
> **❞**

Lando's charity challenge passes the £10k mark so he keeps his part of the bargain, Team Lando Instagram, March 2020.

> "

I don't mind if people see me [as handsome] but I never think of myself like that.

> "

The (undeniably) handsome Lando Norris on being handsome, GQ, January 2023.

"

I want to say a big thank you to all the fans for voting for me. This has been my second time being able to accept this beautiful trophy. The first was during COVID in 2020, but I don't really count that, so this feels like my first.

"

Lando accepts his Autosport's 2023 British Competition Driver of the Year award (voted for by fans) in December 2023.

"

I love it, especially if it's a fan-voted thing. It's just awesome to read, as a normal guy, that there's so many people that support me. But it wouldn't change the way I approach things or change who I am or be a big ego-booster. I try not to think about it too much.

"

Lando reflects on being named the most popular driver among female and Gen-Z fans in 2021, following a 150,000-person F1 fan survey, GQ, January 2023.

"

It's a different life. A lonely
one in many respects. But I've
never been one to say, 'I wish
I could go back and change it.'
I'm very, very lucky to be
a Formula 1 driver. I would
never complain.

"

On life in the fast lane, The Telegraph, June 2024,

"

I love to listen. It might not
be something I'm necessarily
giving input on, but because
I love racing, the more I can
know about, that's a good thing.
I'm a perfectionist. I try as hard
as I can to be a better driver.

"

On the importance of being a good listener,
planetf1.com, January 2023.

"

I think Weetabix and full-fat milk is what it is all about.

"

The breakfast of champions, The Sun, September 2018.

❝

Well, it's looks like I've a love-hate thing going on with Monaco.

❞

On not being sure how to feel about Monaco as an F2 driver, Sky Sports, December 2018.

"

You're never going to please everyone. There are people that support you and people that don't... I know I'm doing the best I can.

"

Lando on the impossibility of pleasing all of the people, all of the time, Sky Sports, January 2023.

"

I just didn't know how to deal with it. I kept all of it inside and it really hurt my self-belief and self-confidence, which got to an all-time low. I doubted myself: Am I good enough to be in Formula 1? Can I come back from this?

"

Lando on his mental health struggles throughout 2019 and 2020, formula1.com, January 2023.

"

A few people said that I had saved their life. That hits you pretty hard.

"

On his openness about mental health issues and the effect it had on others, GQ, January 2023.

"

It's something obviously a lot of drivers do. With just how racing is, you've seen with a lot of drivers how quickly things can go downhill. I still have to look after my life and things for my future, so that's why.

"

On his decision to swap Woking for Monaco for tax reasons, BBC, November 2021.

"

If everything stopped in real life, I would still be very happy to race on a simulator.

"

On his back-up plan, GQ, August 2020.

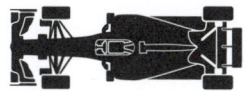

“

Get him away from
that microphone, now.
It's bedtime. You're
supposed to be in bed now,
this is bad parenting.

”

*Lando playfully chides a young audience member
who claimed Max Verstappen was the fastest driver
during a live-stream interview, Daily Express,
January 2025.*

> **"**
>
> I've made my mistakes, and, at the same time, I've learned a lot from those mistakes.
>
> **"**

Lando on his 2024 season performances,
Daily Express, January 2025.

66

It's a stupid thing to do to put your life in danger with cars driving around. It's a very selfish thing to do at the same time because of the consequences it has on the person driving a car if something happened.

99

Lando speaks out on the Just Stop Oil protesters risking their lives on the Silverstone track to get their message across, BBC, July 2023.

159

"

I remember when I took the lead off
the line last year, how cool it was.
I had a moment where I thought,
damn, I'm leading the British Grand
Prix! I remember coming around
Luffield [corner] and looking to the
fans, and seeing them cheering...
That's the biggest thing, genuinely.
The effect that they have. As a
feeling, not just as a thought. It puts
a smile on your face, on the inside
of your helmet. Like, 'Wow.'

"

On how racing on home soil inspires him,
The Telegraph, June 2024.

"

I like the feeling of driving through the gates, through the crowds. There's no place like Silverstone for that, especially for McLaren. I'm sure it's the same for Ferrari at Imola or Monza. It's exciting. It gets the blood going. I did the same last year, driving a McLaren Senna. I want to drive a classic car this year. Maybe a Shelby, or a Cobra...

"

There's no place like home – and Lando did end up arriving in a chromed Shelby Cobra! The Telegraph, July 2024.

CHAPTER
SEVEN

Future Fantastic

After pushing Max Verstappen all the way in 2024, many believed 2025 and beyond would belong to Lando Norris and McLaren...

"

Lando is the favourite for next year now to win the championship.

"

Nico Rosberg shows his faith in Lando,
Sky Sports, December 2024.

66

That's the aim. That's what I would love more than anything: to be the guy – or at least being a big part of – bringing McLaren from where they were three or four years ago at the very bottom all the way back to the very top. And to be there that whole journey, I think that's more special than hopping to another team and winning a race all of a sudden.

99

Lando sees the bigger picture and belts up for the journey ahead, The Standard, March 2022.

FACT

In January 2024 Lando re-signed with McLaren on a "multi-year" contract extension.

With his Australian teammate Oscar Piastri also signing a new long-term contract in March 2025, McLaren's superstar line-up is locked in.

66

It's been a year where, actually, I've been pretty proud of my performance. Proud of performing under the pressure that we've been under, delivering when I have.

99

Lando reflects on finishing behind
Max Verstappen in the 2024 Drivers' Championship,
BBC's F1 Back at Base podcast, January 2025.

"

I've made my mistakes, and,
at the same time, I've learned
a lot from those mistakes.
So for us to go into next year,
going, 'We have what it takes,
we have a car'... I believe I'm
a good enough driver and I've
got everything it takes.

"

On learning from a challenging 2024, BBC's
F1 Back at Base podcast, January 2025.

> "
>
> I have faith in McLaren,
> I have faith in the guys I work
> with, the whole team.
>
> "

*Whether Lando stays a McLaren driver for his
whole career remains to be seen, but his relationship
with the team has always been strong,
Sky Sports, November 2022.*

"

He has shown raw
speed on a level I would
say even with a Max
Verstappen... it's very,
very phenomenal and
it's world champion-like.

"

Nico Rosberg on Lando's natural abilities,
Sky Sports, December 2024.

66

We are the team to beat.
The car is flying. There
will be tracks where we
are even better.

99

On the strong start to the 2025 season,
The Guardian, March 2025.

66

Potentially, there was
a chance to beat him in
Canada. So two races that
I finished second and he's
won. But Max needs to
stop winning in order to
achieve that!

99

On overcoming his current main rival,
formula1.com, June 2024.

"

We can do it. You know, if I just made some better decisions in Canada, and if I had a better start today, we could have won two races. And I know there's a lot of – and there kind of always has been a lot of – 'shoulda, woulda, couldas', but we have what it takes. It's just about putting it all together.

Lando's view on what it will take to come out on top, formula1.com, June 2024.

66

I need to just tidy up a few little bits and we'll be on top.

99

On what is needed to win the ultimate prize, formula1.com, June 2024.

> **66**
>
> **Pit Wall:** *Who do you think we are racing? Just Max?*
>
> **Lando Norris:** *I think we are racing everyone, especially the car ahead.*
>
> **99**

Lando's dryly funny radio exchange with his team during the 2024 Dutch Grand Prix, formula1.com, August 2024.

" This guy's mega. "

Zak Brown's succinct summary
of Lando's abilities, BBC, March 2025.

❝

From the outside,
I understand why people
think it hasn't been.
And I completely...
almost agree with it!

❞

*On undertsanding why, from the outside, the 2024
season might not have seemed as good as it should have
therace.com, November 2024.*

"

I'm excited to go into 2025 knowing I've learned a lot; I've improved a lot and I'm ready to bring the fight to everyone.

"

Fighting talk, formula1.com, January 2025.

> **"**
>
> I'm happy that I stuck through the harder times when I could have picked an easier route out of it, could have gone to different teams. The team understand that too, the journey that we've been on together, and I think they appreciate that, which probably makes me the happiest out of all of it.
>
> **"**

*On reaping the rewards of being loyal to McLaren,
gpfans.com, November 2024.*

"

If all of sudden we go
into next year and
in the middle of the
championship it's me and
Max and Lewis, I don't
think there will be as
much Mr Nice Guy. That's
just the way it works.

"

On having to toughen up if he wants to be a
champion, BBC, November 2021.

"

Confidence is something
I've struggled with in the past.
And probably I've only built
enough up throughout this
season to go, 'I'm confident that
I'm a good enough driver to win
a championship next year,' and
I can bring a fight to whoever
wants to fight me for it.

"

On his newfound confidence, crash.net,
February 2025.

66

It would have been easy for [the team] to get back and just go, 'Ah, we're good, we've done it now. Let's just relax.' They've done the opposite. They've gone, 'We want even more,' and they've worked even harder to try and find new things for this year. They've turned these expectations into positive things, into more motivation and more drive to want it again.

99

On how McLaren are always striving for more, The Mirror, February 2025.

66

As much as I want to win the constructors' every single year, the selfish one is to win the Drivers' Championship. You need a good team behind you, and that's exactly what I've got.

99

Lando's personal mission, The Mirror, February 2025.

66

I came close-ish [in 2024], I was still always a bit far behind, but I could smell it. I had that feeling of like, 'Okay, this is kind of what it's like.' It was within reach. [For 2025], I need to fix a few things, work on some things, and come back stronger, and that's what I'm ready to do.

99

On being within touching distance of the championship, racefans.net, January 2025.

"

There might be some benefits in the race for those [2026] regulations, there might be some things that are worse. The type of racing you're going to get is probably quite different... I don't think anyone knows exactly how it's going to pan out.

"

On the unknown future of the 2026 regulation change, autosport.com, June 2024.

"

I know exactly which
[team] I would love to
go to – it's the team that
everyone wants to be
part of at some point in
their career – but I'm very
happy with McLaren.

"

*Lando cheekily hints at a future in red overalls,
planetf1.com, March 2025.*

"

Obviously I'm doing something right.

"

Hard to disagree! GP Racing, September 2018.

"

We still have a lot of work to do but every race is an opportunity.

"

On continually working hard to be the best,
autosport.com, October 2021.

"

I don't think there's any point going for second or third.

"

Lando's winning mentality was clear in F2,
ESPN, January 2018.

> **❝**
>
> # I want to go down in the history books with what I've achieved.
>
> **❞**

On the legacy he's aiming for, The Standard, July 2019.

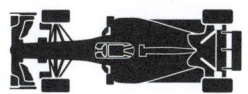

> "
>
> There's 20 of us in the world, and I'm one of those 20 who gets to live one of the coolest lives I would say you can live with great people. So many perks, get to travel the world and just race cars.
>
> "

On living the dream, racefans.net, September 2023.

"

I'd like to get one of those.

"

Lando points to a replica
Driver's Championship Trophy as he leads
a journalist through McLaren HQ,
GQ, January 2023.